Get Up, Get Out
&
Get Some Healing

Chris E. James

ISBN: 9798354844715

DEDICATION

I'd like to dedicate to this book to the people I love the most. To my two big brothers, Roderick McCoy and Jimmy McCoy, I love you and I can only imagine what you've had to encounter inside those walls. I hope and pray that your mind and heart stay strong and that you hold on to the peace inside you. Don't be defeated by that which incarcerates your body. What we just endured with the loss of our mama ain't easy but as long as we stick together on this healing journey, we will be good.

To my nieces, Taliyah McCoy, Ronisha McCoy and Zaniah Hudson, I know all of you have experienced hurt that you didn't ask for but I want you to know that healing is possible. You deserve to be happy. You deserve good things and a truly peaceful life. I really want that for all of you. But until you want it for yourself, it will be out of reach. So decide that you want it badly and get it.

To my little cousin, Ricky Moore, you were just comforting

me four months ago when I loss my mama. You said to me, "Cuz, I know I'ma need you soon too." I doubt either of us imagined you'd be losing your mom soon after. But like I've already told you face to face, I GOT YOU. Your healing journey is yours but I'm always right here to support in all the ways I can.

Lastly, I have to of course dedicate this book to my mama, SHARON DENISE HARDAWAY, the realist one to ever to grace this earth. My mama was my best friend, my first love, my first cheerleader, my biggest fan, my rock. Although she has transitioned in a physical sense, I trust that she is with me and all of us she loved. I love you mama and I am eternally grateful for all the love you poured in me.

CONTENTS

FOREWORD

BY DR. CURTIS D. JASPER, PHD

As a community, social, and relational licensed psychologist, I'm not only fortunate enough to work in quite a few arenas but I also get to work with many outstanding, highly functional, and creative individuals doing amazing work for themselves and others, locally, nationally, and globally. Chris James is one such individual!

I met Mr. James a few years ago and immediately experienced his brilliance, creativity, passion, and compassion. He is a rare individual who actually walks the walk and not just talks the talk. Chris and I have teamed up on a number of projects and community events. When he mentioned his new book, I was excited to share in his joy.

I AM grateful that Mr. James asked me to be included in his book. Not only did I learn lots of new things and brushed up on lots of things I should have retained from many years ago, the manuscript flowed like the perfect lyrics over a dope beat. Chris starts off by informing the reader that there's a relationship that must be developed between oneself and one's emotions. He brilliantly states that emotions serve a purpose and are messengers delivering a message.

It's my strong belief Mr. James was not intending for this to be a typical self-help "salesy" type of book (as a matter of fact, I know it wasn't!). His writing approach is very conversationally-friendly, but highly informative. It's filled with lots of imagery, humor, pop-culture references, personal anecdotes, formal definitions, resources, written activities, and lots of transparency.

I read the entire manuscript in one sitting and it felt as if Chris and I were having one of our monthly 'Fella's Mixers' group conversations. The written exercises will help the reader embody certain feelings and emotions as well as gain an initial feeling of how to begin to retrain the nervous system on one's own personal healing journey. The easily digestible metaphors, examples, and analogies demonstrates Mr. James' superb writing skills and abilities whereas the average reader will continue to be engaged and captivated to the very last page.

Chris James' call-to-action for a stronger more aggressive mental health awareness campaign is highly commendable, needed, and necessary. Not only is Mr. James an advocate for mental health awareness, he's on his own healing journey of which he explicitly shares details for the reader. There's a chapter in the book where Chris states "…my brothers imprisonment had also imprisoned me emotionally." Not only was this a profound statement but a testament to many of us in the Black community who are and have experienced the same events.

The brief, generable but informative overview of mental health disorders, definitions of emotions, resources, written exercises, and specific questions directed to the reader puts you in the mind of a user-friendly webinar of which you know is not only highly beneficial but fun to learn.

It goes without saying that I highly recommend you read this book more than once, as well as take notes and buy a few copies for your friends and loved-ones. Allow yourself to initiate a new relationship between YOU and your EMOTIONS! It'll change your life and those around you.

In honor of Mr. Chris James, I'll end with his own words— He "broke down the process of healing in a very practical way." He easily delivered on that intention and much, much more.

Thank you, Chris James, for allowing your truth, your honesty, your vulnerability, and your personal growth and development to serve as a manual unlike any other "self-help" or trendy "Mental Health" book on the market today.

Dr. Curtis D. Jasper, PhD

Psychologist

Author | Speaker | Mental Health Advocate | Emotional Wellness Expert | Corporate Consultant | Lecturer | Educator

www.DrCurtisDJasper.com

GET OFF THE COUCH

THE INTRODUCTION

I can't deny it. I'm super excited that you decided to come on this journey with me. I hope today is a good day for you. I hope your world is light. I know how heavy it can sometimes be. I hope today your world is full of light. I know how dark it can be on certain days in certain ways.

Question, if I may ask. What made you open this book? Obviously, you can't tell me the answer, but I would like you to answer it for yourself. Is there some healing that needs to happen in your life? It is my assumption that every single human living on this Earth has something to heal from, or at some point, they will. It's just one of those unfortunate hard truths we should face. I began writing this book when I was at the height of my healing journey. I had just lost my mother. It was legitimately the hardest thing I've ever experienced in my life. Grief showed me no mercy.

Kendrick Lamar shared in his song *Mother I Sober*, "You never experienced grief until you experienced it sober." That line hit home for me. Every day for at least a month after my mother's funeral, I was either high or intoxicated. I was doing everything in my power to avoid the feeling of grief. I was terrified to face it, honestly. I used drugs and alcohol to run. The numbness helped me to escape most days, but on other days, grief would snatch me up and leave me balling with tears in the corner of the bathroom. I knew I couldn't keep running, so one day, I challenged myself not to. The alcohol and marijuana had to get out of my car while I took this ride alone. I was nervous that I might become dependent on these things long-term if I didn't slow down. So, I accepted the challenge.

Maria Hampton, an artist and friend of mine, once spoke about the importance of embracing your darkness. The darkness is just as much a part of us as the light. The reality is that we have a relationship with all of our emotions, and they all serve a purpose. It's up to us to foster those relationships so we can understand the roles of those emotions. By doing so, we can more effectively manage how they impact our lives. In accepting my self-appointed challenge, I spent some very intimate time with my grief; yes, it was dark. It was not at all paradise in the park. It was soul-wrenching and destructive. It was exhausting, like long days of heavy lifting with no break. The pain was excruciating, but it was necessary. Like gold that has gone through fire, I came out refined and renewed. In facing my darkness, my grief, I realized it was me who gave that emotion the power to be this monster of a thing.

After spending time with it, I came to learn that it wasn't this huge beastly creature I had made it out to be. But in fact, it was just another thing that needed some attention, and it wasn't all that scary, nor was it out to harm me. As a result of facing my grief, I can honestly say I am stronger and better than I've ever been. I'm not at all the same man I was a year ago. I am healthier mentally, physically, spiritually, and emotionally.

Days before my mother passed away, I texted all my friends, "I don't know what's about to happen, but whatever happens, please don't let me spiral and lose my mind. I'ma need y'all." I was issuing a fire signal before I even needed rescuing. I was scared of what grief might do. I've seen what it's done to people. I've seen what hitting rock bottom and living with untreated trauma has done to the strongest and the healthiest. I didn't want that to happen to me. I didn't want to look up five years later and still be stuck on the couch.

Throughout this book, I'll speak a lot about being on the couch. "On the Couch" is where we reside when we are mentally and emotionally incarcerated by our trauma, and we have yet to get up and begin doing something towards our healing. I have spent quite some time on this metaphorical couch myself. After my eight-year relationship ended, I was on the couch. When my two oldest brothers got sentenced to twenty-five and forty years in prison, I was on the couch. When I went six months without income, I was on the couch. And, of course, when I lost my mom, I was back on the couch. It was never fun. Nothing good ever happens here. You only become infected and even more sick the longer you stay on the couch.

The title of the book is inspired by Outkast's 1994 hit song, "Git Up, Git Out." Through the speakers, Outkast and Goodie Mobb gave us an upbeat yet poetic instruction to GET UP, GET OUT and GET SOMETHING and to not allow the days of our lives to pass us by. In this book, my message is very similar. It is my hope that if you are still on the couch, by the time you finish this read, become inspired enough to GET UP, GET OUT and GET SOME HEALING.

I don't expect getting off the couch will be or should be easy. It is hard work, but we all know that hard work is the most rewarding. And I know firsthand that healing is not a destination but a journey you and I will forever be traveling on. As you travel through these pages, I hope I offer a comprehensive and digestible approach to the healing process so that you may be more motivated to get off the couch and begin your journey to healing. I want you to be whole because you deserve more than you probably know. I want that for you more than I can ever show you. And I believe and trust that healing will cover you in due time.

Before you move on to the first chapter, I'd like to encourage you not to rush this read. Take your time. Study the information. Pause and come back to it. Take advantage of the exercises and challenges presented. Use this book as a resource, a tool. This information will only contribute to your growth. Now, let's get to it and let the work begin. Maybe, this poem will inspire you a little more.

I Prayed For You

|Get Off the Couch|

It's been a while since I last prayed for me
but last night I prayed for you.
I prayed for your sanity to remain a resident.
I noticed that depression moved in.
Made a house out of your heart
A backyard out of your mind.

I've watched happy knocking at your door but you aint got
up off the couch to answer.
You and anxiety and grief been watching re-runs of your
downfalls
Depression has lowered the blinds and closed the curtains
Allowing no light in your house
Your heart has become a dark space
A stranger to the other side of night.
You've become slave to a sunken place
It appears you've become numb to the feeling
to feeling.
Anything
and everything is ugly
Nothing possesses the same beauty it once did
according to the windows, the eyes you see out of.
Spring is no different from autumn or winter
Every day is cold
Leaves always fall
Grass aint ever green
Flowers don't ever blossom to bloom
Aint no sunshine
even when she aint gone.
I hear depression introduced you to suicide.
Say y'all spend late nights together
Talking about all the ways to visit death.
Like taking flights off the top of the bridge
or driving into a lake
or cutting across your wrist into your veins

as if death was a mathematician and could somehow solve
your problems.

Last night I prayed for you
until my knees were bleeding from blisters
But when God showed up
he said you wouldn't even let him in.
Told him he aint welcome there no more.
Said your company slammed the door in his face.
Who the hell is misery anyway?
He ought to learn some manners.
I heard he don't clean up after himself.
Was only supposed to stay a night but somehow now got a
toothbrush in your bathroom.
You need to learn to speak up for yourself and kick dude
nem out your house.

Every day it seems a party is being thrown in your mind,
your backyard is a wreck
Full of baggage filled with trash and burdens that don't
even belong to you.
But you seem to always be the only one left to clean it up.

Aint you tired of having that reoccurring dream?
You know the one when it's flooding in your house
then you notice all the water is actually your own tears
And the life jacket is actually full of weights but you put it
on anyway

and you drown.
Aint you tired of drowning in your own tears.
How long til you stop playing victim and finally win.
How long til you finally wade in these waters and finally
swim.
Dry land aint far. The shore is right there.

The sun been ready to set
But you gotta stop this rain
There is a rainbow after your storm
with a pot of gold and dancing Leprechauns at the bottom.
Can't you hear the ringing of church bells and choirs
singing
trying to caste out all your demons
I hear em screaming
Gasping for air,
Stop letting em suck up all of your air.

Yo, I hear happy misses you.
Said it really wants to move back in
and be friends like y'all used to be
back before you allowed depression to be your roommate.
I hear he don't pay rent anyway.
Just smoke a lot of weed, leave the ashes and seeds all
around the house.
Might as well kick him out.
You know happy always provided groceries
filled you up with nourishment.

Nowadays you so empty,
starving to be fed again
to be happy again.

The choice is yours.
Happy is at your door.
All you gotta do is, GET OFF THIS COUCH and answer
and let it in.
Choose happy.

LISTEN TO POEM ON YOUTUBE

CHAPTER 1

WHAT IS MENTAL HEALTH?

Mental Health? At some point, you've probably heard someone mention it. In today's society, it is a popular conversation. Now more than ever, as a culture, we are becoming more aware and vocal about mental health. In my experience in academia, I've heard students as young as eight years old describe their own mental health as depression. Over twenty years ago, a child that young may have felt depressed, but they didn't know to identify it as a mental health issue.

Although many people today are hyper-aware and knowledgeable of mental health, there are so many more who do not understand this subject matter much at all. So, what is it?

"Mental Health is a state of well-being in which an individual: realizes their own abilities, can cope with the normal stressors of life, can work productively and fruitfully, and contribute to their community" (National Council for Mental Wellbeing).

"Mental health includes our emotional, psychological, and social well-being. It affects how we think, feel, and act. It also helps determine how we handle stress, relate to others, and make choices. Mental health is important at every stage of life, from childhood and adolescence through adulthood. Over the course of your life, if you experience mental health problems, your thinking, mood, and behavior could be affected.

Many factors contribute to mental health problems, including:
- Biological factors, such as genes or brain chemistry
- Life experiences, such as trauma or abuse
- Family history of mental health problems

Mental health problems are common, but help is available. People with mental health problems can get better, and many recover completely." - MentalHealth.Gov.

Mental health problems can arise commonly, similarly to a cold or a headache, after a long day. But just like a cold can be treated, mental health illnesses can sometimes forgo simple remedies; other times, more extreme measures have to be taken, but there is most often always a remedy.

What are some things that might negatively impact your mental health?

1. Participating in unhealthy or negative conversations that have no resolve or intention to mean good.

2. Participating in activities that you wholeheartedly don't want to do, but you do it to make others happy.

3. Smoking cigarettes or marijuana, drinking alcohol, or any drug to suppress certain feelings or thoughts that make you uncomfortable to experience when you're completely sober.

4. Having sex to suppress certain feelings or thoughts that make you uncomfortable.

5. Resorting to verbal abuse, aggressive or loud responses, or physical behaviors when an uncomfortable topic or situation arises.

6. Resorting to silence or being stubborn when an uncomfortable topic or situation arises.

7. Someone saying or doing something repeatedly (or once) to you that you do not explicitly welcome or invite that creates discomfort or confusion.

8. Losing someone you love to death or a relationship ending.

9. Being rejected, abandoned, or not included.

10. Not being appreciated or recognized.

11. Holding in your emotions and not expressing them.

12. Not eating healthy foods.

13. Gaining weight or not being satisfied with your appearance.

14. Not liking the person you are and comparing yourself to others.

15. Not having the things society has influenced you to have; a spouse, a high-earning job, home ownership, etc.

16. Living in poverty.

17. Living in a messy home or being surrounded by

disorganization.

18. Not being in a healthy and happy relationship that grows you.

19. Not making progress.

20. Not getting an adequate amount of sleep.

As you observe this list and think of many other things that may have impacted your mental health in a negative way, make a note of them. It is also worth mentioning that we have a level of control over many of the things listed. Not control over the fact that some of them already happened, but we have ultimate control over the power we give said experiences. We also have control over our reactions to these situations. Some of these things, we have the ability to change completely. Ancient Philosopher, Epictetus, shares that we will get closer to mastering life once we accept the things that we cannot control and no longer try to control them.

Ask yourself, *Am I mentally healthy?* This isn't something you can look in the mirror and discover. You have to look internally to answer this question. I encourage you right now, at this very moment, to check in with yourself. Ask yourself, *How do I feel?* Then ask yourself, *Why do I feel this way,* and *how often do I feel this way? Does my mood or behaviors change when I feel this way?* Ask yourself, *How do I respond when I am emotionally charged; sad, frustrated, angry, irritated, tired, anxious, excited, happy, etc.?*

Are you mentally healthy? Do you have the capacity to recognize and identify when your mental health is being affected? Most times, when people aren't mentally healthy, they don't ever think anything is wrong with them.

Everything is fine, so they say from their mouth, even when tornados and storms are raging inside of them. But because they have grown so used to not knowing that these feelings aren't normal or healthy, they accept it as just the way things are sometimes. Have you experienced traumatic situations and just kept going without ever addressing what you think or feel about the experience? I once had a friend who never cried or expressed any emotion. I thought *He must really have his stuff together to be able to experience such tragic things and not cry or get mad, and just be able to walk away like nothing just happened.* I later discovered he was just numb, desensitized, and avoided ever feeling or connecting too deeply to experiences that affected him emotionally because it was easier not to deal with the discomfort.

I am telling you right now that it does not contribute to your mental health in a good way to avoid feeling. Do not suppress feelings or thoughts that inspire discomfort. When you put these feelings and thoughts in emotional storage boxes, they always find a way to pop out of other boxes like a JACK IN THE BOX toy. Boom, there goes that daddy issue from your childhood popping out in your adult relationship with your boss. Boom, there goes that sexual trauma popping out while you're attempting to be intimate with your wife or husband. Boom, there goes that abandonment issue popping out when your best friend wants to hang out with their new friends for a night instead of you.

Are you mentally healthy? You really have to ask yourself

this and be honest about it. Lay it all out on the table. Let's call it a MENTAL HEALTH AUDIT. Take out all the receipts, spread them out on the table, and observe closely how you have actually shown up in the world mentally and emotionally.

I think of being mentally healthy the same way I look at being physically strong. How does a person know when they're physically strong? One might say it is when they are simply able to lift and move heavy things. I apply that same concept to mental health. A person who is mentally healthy is one who has the ability to cope with heavy emotional and mental trauma. Can a physically strong person have moments of weakness, moments when they cannot lift or move certain heavy things? Of course. And these moments do not make them overall weak, but it actually means they are even stronger if and when they are wise enough to ask for help to lift what is too heavy to carry alone. So yes, you can be mentally healthy and have days when you struggle with your mental health, but the ability to recognize that you need help and to actually seek it means you have a high level of mental strength.

So again, I ask, are you mentally healthy? If so, great. Keep doing the work. If you're not sure, let's begin doing the work. If you've opened this book and made it this far, it's obvious that you're ready to get in the gym and get your reps in. We all deserve to be healthy mentally and to heal from all the pain life has authored onto our pages.

<u>Something to Remember:</u>

A Mental Health Challenge/Struggle is when:

a. A major change in a person's feeling, thinking, or acting changes.

b. It interferes with a person's ability to live their life.

c. The interference does not go away quickly and lasts longer than the typical emotions or reactions would be expected to.

CHAPTER 2

WHAT IS MENTAL ILLNESS REALLY?

"Yesterday, I was mentally ill. Today, I am mentally healthy."

Mental illness can work like that in many cases. In other cases, not so much. Mental illness can come and go, and sometimes it lingers indefinitely. Mental illness isn't like a common cold or a tummy ache. It's not something you can cure with an over-the-counter drug or a hot toddy. Mental illness is not something a doctor can walk into the room and immediately recognize or diagnose. It is a complex Rubix cube that can change its form at any moment. You may have figured out one, but the next one won't be like the last. Mental illness comes in many colors, and no case or experience is ever the same. Each person experiences mental illness differently, even if the mental illness is similar. And although mental illness isn't the most common thing to understand or identify right away, it doesn't mean that we can't all do the work required to have the knowledge to better equip ourselves to understand, manage, and support mental illness when it is present in our lives or around us. We often have no control over when or how mental illness comes into our lives.

What is mental illness? The *National Alliance of Mental Illness* defines mental illness as a condition that affects a person's thinking, feeling, behavior or mood. These conditions deeply impact day-to-day living and may also affect the ability to relate to others. Mental illness can be caused by many factors. It can be caused by biological factors such as genes or brain chemistry. It can be caused by life experiences such as trauma or abuse. It can also come about because of a family history of mental health problems.

The *Alabama Department of Mental Health* shared in a presentation called "Understanding the Biology of Mental Illness" that "The term mental illness clearly indicates there is a problem with the brain. In order to understand mental illness, it is good to understand the brain and how it works.

The brain controls all the actions of the body. It is often referred to as a person's master control center. The brain has many functions that can be categorized into six components. The first is thinking or cognition. The second is perception or sensing. The third function of the brain is emotions. Signaling is the fourth function of the brain. The fifth is physical functions. The sixth and last function of the brain is behavior. Everything that we do, all of our behavior, is controlled by the brain. Our behavior is dependent on all the other things that the brain does. Most functions of the brain are interrelated. If something happens in one part of the brain, it will often show up in one or more other parts.

For example, if you're feeling sad, it can affect your mood, physical state, and behavior. Your stomach and head can hurt. You can think negative thoughts and avoid being around your friends. In the presentation, they also share that mental illness happens when something in the brain isn't working properly or when the brain gets sick. It is said that a number of things can be happening inside the brain such as:

a. A specific part of the brain isn't working well.

b. A specific part of the brain is working in the wrong way.

c. A brain network could be disrupted.

d. Neurochemical messengers aren't working properly.

What does it mean to be ill? It means that you are not in full health; or sick. To be mentally ill is just that; a lack of being in full health, being sick mentally. In this case, it matters for the person experiencing this level of illness to be cared for just as one might care for a child experiencing the flu, a broken arm, or a common cold. People who are mentally ill should be thought of as fragile, and they should be handled with compassion and emotional caution. We all should do the work to understand the signs of mental illness so we can recognize it if and when it arises within our own lives or in someone's life near us. It is common for individuals to experience mental illness or to see it and brush it off simply because they don't have the basic knowledge to understand it or the language to give it a name. And when we aren't able to give it a name, the illness becomes unclaimed and ignored for what it is.

In recent years, we've seen police officers handle mentally ill individuals with aggression that fatally resulted in murder because they deemed their illness-affected behavior as noncompliance when in fact, it was not. According to a study released by the *Treatment Advocacy Center*, "People with untreated mental illness are 16 times more likely to be killed during a police encounter than other civilians approached or stopped by law enforcement."

This is tragic. Being ignorant of mental illness doesn't only result in atrocious acts like murder, either. Sometimes, the result is losing a relationship with someone you love because you were unable to realize their mental illness. Other times we find ourselves responding to friends, family, co-workers, or random people on the street who are battling mental illness with culturally influenced microaggressions.

A Deeper Look into Microaggressions

Unfortunately, society has done a great job at creating stigmas around the topic of mental illness. Over the years, I've heard people with mental illnesses be described as crazy, retarded, not right, sick in the head, out of whack, too emotional, disturbed, and many more. These descriptions have been used in a way that dismisses and invalidates the person and their mental health challenges. And frankly, it is not okay.

What are microaggressions? Webster defines microaggressions as a statement, actions, or incidents regarded as an instance of indirect, subtle, or unintentional discrimination against members of a marginalized group such as a racial or ethnic minority. In this case, the marginalized group happens to be the mentally ill. Here are some examples of microaggressions:

Statements:
"There you go acting crazy."

"Why are you sweating and acting nervous?"

"Ain't nothing wrong with you. Relax."

"How can somebody like you be depressed?"

"Stop stressing over this."

Actions & Scenarios:

1. Laughing at someone with mental health struggles.

2. Chastising or being critical of a person's inability to perform as they normally would.

3. Taking a call or checking texts while a person is in the middle of an episode.

According to *Medical News Today*, "Microaggressions can take several forms." They may be:

- Verbal: A verbal microaggression is a comment or question that is hurtful or stigmatizing to a marginalized group or person. For example, saying, "You're so smart for a woman."

- Behavioral: This involves behaving in a discriminatory or otherwise hurtful way to a marginalized person or group.

For example, when a waiter or bartender ignores a transgender person and instead serves a cisgender person, someone whose biological sex matches their gender identity.

- Environmental: An environmental microaggression is when a subtle discriminatory action occurs within society, for example, when a store or restaurant doesn't have seating space or an entry ramp for a person in a wheelchair.

Take a moment and write down some microaggressions that you can think of as it relates to mental illness:

Mental Illness and More Stigmas

Is mental illness dangerous? It absolutely can be. It can be dangerous for the person experiencing it and for the person in observation. Anything can be dangerous when we don't understand it enough to manage it, support it, or respond to it properly. A gun, for example, isn't necessarily dangerous unless it makes contact with someone who is ignorant of what it is and handles it without caution or care. A fire is not dangerous until someone allows it to be in environments without containment, and it is given the opportunity to spread out of control.

I've been driving for a long time. My mom started giving me driving lessons when I was twelve years old in the Lynch Drive Elementary school parking lot after hours. With about twenty years of driving experience, I can confidently say I am a great driver, but even for me, driving can become dangerous. I often tell people that you're taking a risk every time you decide to get in a car. Because the moment you or someone else on the road loses focus even for a second, driving can become dangerous.

According to the *National Safety Council*, in 2020, as many as 42,060 people are estimated to have died in motor vehicle crashes. Does that mean that driving is dangerous? My answer is no. But if we are not focused on all the right precautions while we travel up and down the roads, danger can smack us at any time. Even when we are doing all the right things, we can find ourselves being rear-ended out of nowhere. So just like driving, you could know everything you need to know about your mind. You could have read every book there is about psychology, but even still, the dangers of mental illness can rear-end you and crash into your "perfect" life without warning. So no, crashes can't always be avoided. Neither can mental illness. But if we do the work to be knowledgeable on how to handle these crashes in our lives, the impact won't sting as much. Is mental illness dangerous? My answer is NO! But to be clear, even the simplest, everyday activities and behaviors can be dangerous when we lack the knowledge needed.

Everything is perspective. When I was a child, Rottweilers and Pitbull dogs were monsters in my eyes. When I used to ride my bike and walk to school, there were these two Rottweilers at this old lady's house on Prothro Street. The two huge dogs would bark and jump on the fence every time I passed there. I always ran or took off on my bike because I was terrified of what might happen if they ever got loose. Then I remember the day one of them hopped the fence and got free. I took off so fast. It came running after me. I couldn't take off fast enough, so I jumped off the bike and stood on one side of it to protect myself, while the

Rottweiler stood on the other side of the bike, just barking loud as it possibly could. Here I was, scared out of my mind feeling as if death was inches from my life. All of a sudden, this pale old lady came outside and called the dog's name like she was yelling at her child, and immediately his barking ceased, and he went back to his yard, and my life was saved.

What I learned later in life is that the Rottweiler wasn't really a monster. It was actually just a bigger and louder version of the little puppy it was a year prior, soft and cuddly. But it was my fear that empowered this false narrative of the dog, and it was also my fear that hyped up that dog to believe it was more powerful than it actually was. The pale old lady wasn't big or strong, but she understood the big loud dog, which made her able to handle the very thing I feared. To this day, I sometimes still flinch when I encounter dogs. In 2017, I went to New Orleans and stayed at my friend Carolyn's home. She has a German Shepard that's easily taller than me if it stands on its back legs. I walked in, and the dog started barking. I wanted to jump on the couch. To my surprise, the young lady that came with me on the trip got down on one knee, opened her arms, and summoned the dog over to her. The dog stopped barking, came over to her, and rolled over on its back as she rubbed his belly. It wasn't magic or voodoo that helped her get along with the dog. It was just a simple understanding of the dog that allowed her the privilege of not fearing it.

And to be clear, I only feared this dog because I was ignorant. But now that I've done the work to understand, I can say I am no longer fearful of dogs. Is mental illness a monster? Absolutely not. But if you allow yourself to remain ignorant, it will be a false image you hang on the walls of your mind and that my friend is not okay.

What is your relationship with mental illness? I'd like to think that most people have had an encounter on some level. My relationship with mental illness is a very close one. We've lived together for a long time now. At first, I didn't realize *what* it was. It happened when my brothers both were sentenced to twenty-five and forty-year prison sentences. I was sixteen years old. My mother and I lived on 405 West 24th Street in North Little Rock, Arkansas. I recall sitting in my room attempting to write my brothers a letter, and out of nowhere, instead of words filling the page, my tears did. I couldn't stop crying. Fast forward to my freshman year of college. I was on a date at Chilis with Nikki Elebeke. Everything was going perfectly. She was laughing. I was laughing. Then we got to a part of the night where we began to talk about family. I remember it like it was yesterday. It was my turn, and the moment I made mention of my brothers, the tears came rushing down my face like broken levees in New Orleans, and I couldn't even stop them enough to continue the date. That was the day I truly faced my depression.

I realized I had no control of the deep sadness inside me because I had not done the work to truly acknowledge that my brother's imprisonment had also imprisoned me emotionally. I spent so long suppressing the emotional trauma that I had become mentally ill and infected. This is a result of allowing the sore to fester, to go untreated.

A Deeper Look at Mental Illness

Famous rapper from Memphis once said, "Women lie, men lie, numbers don't lie." Let's take a look at the numbers to have a wider and more in-depth understanding of mental illness and its impact. *The National Association of Mental Illness* has provided us with the following data:

"43.8 million adults experience mental illness within a given year.

1 in 5 adults in America experience mental illness.

Nearly 1 in 25 (10 million) adults in America live with a serious mental illness.

One-half of all chronic mental illness begins by the age of 14; three-quarters by the age of 24.

1 in 100 (2.4 million) American adults live with schizophrenia.

2.6% (6.1 million) of American adults live with bipolar disorder.

6.9% (16 million) of American adults live with major depression.

18.1% (42 million) of American adults live with anxiety

disorders."

CONSEQUENCES

Approximately 10.2 million adults have co-occurring mental health and addiction disorders.

Approximately 26% of homeless adults staying in shelters live with serious mental illnesses.

Approximately 24% of state prisoners have "a recent history of a mental health condition."

IMPACT

Depression is the leading cause of disability worldwide and is a major contributor to the global burden of disease.

Serious mental illness costs America $193.2 billion in lost earnings every year.

Of those who die by suicide, 90% have an underlying mental illness. Suicide is the 10th leading cause of death in the U.S.

TREATMENT IN AMERICA

Nearly 60% of adults with a mental illness didn't receive mental health services in the previous year.

Nearly 50% of youth aged eight-fifteen didn't receive mental health services in the previous year.

African & Hispanic Americans used mental health services at about 1/2 the rate of whites in the past year and Asian Americans at about 1/3 the rate."

Every October, our cities are covered in pink, the roads in our downtown areas are blocked off, millions of dollars are donated for research, and people release balloons for their loved ones, all in the name of breast cancer. And to be clear, I'm all for this movement towards awareness and a cure for breast cancer. But after seeing the numbers above, isn't it painfully obvious that we should begin a movement just as aggressive for mental illness awareness?

Most don't know what mental illnesses are, how to define them, or recognize them when they show up. Here is a list of mental health issues and illnesses and their definitions. We should all do the work to learn about these so we can do a better job at eliminating the stigmas.

The following disorders and illnesses are defined by the

Better Health Channel through the Victorian Government in Australia.

Anxiety Disorders

Anxiety disorders are a group of mental health disorders that includes generalized anxiety disorders, social phobias, specific phobias (for example, agoraphobia and claustrophobia), panic disorders, obsessive-compulsive disorders (OCD), and post-traumatic stress disorders. Untreated anxiety disorders can lead to significant impairment in people's daily lives.

Behavioral and Emotional Disorders in Children

Common behavior disorders in children include oppositional defiant disorder (ODD), conduct disorder (CD), and attention deficit hyperactivity disorder (ADHD). Treatment for these mental health disorders can include therapy, education, and medication.

Bipolar Affective Disorder

Bipolar affective disorder is a type of mood disorder previously referred to as "manic depression." A person with bipolar disorder experiences episodes of mania (elation) and depression. The person may or may not experience psychotic symptoms. The exact cause is unknown, but a genetic predisposition has been clearly established. Environmental stressors can also trigger episodes of this mental illness.

Depression

Depression is a mood disorder characterized by a lowering of mood, loss of interest and enjoyment, and reduced energy. It is not just feeling sad. There are different types and symptoms of depression. There are varying levels of severity and symptoms related to depression. Symptoms of depression can lead to an increased risk of suicidal thoughts or behaviors.

Dissociation and Dissociative Disorders

Dissociation is a mental process where a person disconnects from their thoughts, feelings, memories, or sense of identity. Dissociative disorders include dissociative amnesia, dissociative fugue, depersonalization disorder, and dissociative identity disorder.

Eating Disorders

Eating disorders include anorexia, bulimia nervosa, and other binge eating disorders. Eating disorders affect females and males and can have serious psychological and physical consequences.

Obsessive Compulsive Disorder

Obsessive-compulsive disorder (OCD) is an anxiety disorder. Obsessions are recurrent thoughts, images, or impulses that are intrusive and unwanted. Compulsions are time-consuming and distressing repetitive rituals.

Treatments include cognitive behavior therapy (CBT) and medications.

Paranoia

Paranoia is the irrational and persistent feeling that people are "out to get you." Paranoia may be a symptom of conditions including paranoid personality disorder, delusional (paranoid) disorder, and schizophrenia. Treatment for paranoia includes medications and psychological support.

Post-Traumatic Stress Disorder

Post-traumatic stress disorder (PTSD) is a mental health condition that can develop as a response to people who have experienced any traumatic event. This can be a car or other serious accident, physical or sexual assault, war-related events or torture, or natural disasters such as bushfires or floods.

Psychosis

People affected by psychosis can experience delusions, hallucinations, and confused thinking. Psychosis can occur in a number of mental illnesses, including drug-induced psychosis, schizophrenia, and mood disorders. Medication and psychological support can relieve or even eliminate psychotic symptoms.

Schizophrenia

Schizophrenia is a complex psychotic disorder characterized by disruptions to thinking and emotions and a distorted perception of reality. Symptoms of schizophrenia vary widely but may include hallucinations, delusions, thought disorder, social withdrawal, lack of motivation, and impaired thinking and memory. People with schizophrenia have a high risk of suicide. Schizophrenia is not a split personality.

Congratulations! If you just read this entire chapter, you've successfully made progress towards understanding mental illness and disorders. Hopefully, some of the stigmas you once believed about mental illness and disorders have begun to collapse. In order for us to heal, we must do the work to accept that the thing in front of us, behind us, and inside of us is real. And once we have done the work to acquire the knowledge, we should share it. It would be an injustice to allow anyone around us to remain in lack when we have so much to give.

CHAPTER 3

WHAT IS HEALING
AND WHY SHOULD I DO IT?

In order to define healing, I find it appropriate to define the opposite first. The opposite of being healed is a lot like being in the dark, unable to see what is beyond you clearly. It is cloudy and blurry. It is like driving down a freeway at 10 pm without headlights, no street lights, and pouring rain on your windshield while you wear the darkest shade of sunglasses. When you are not healed, it's a lot like being stuck, unable to move, and you don't even realize you're still in the same place.

Meanwhile, the world around you is constantly in motion.

It's like being numb, not feeling at all, or being limited on what you're able to feel. It's like being a superhero and not being able to use your powers to the fullest. People are staring at you, waiting to be saved, but you're not even able to save yourself. When you're not healed, to be honest, you're not yourself. You're like the characters in the Snicker commercials, but you don't need a Snicker to snap back to yourself; you need access to deeper healing. When you are not healed, you are not whole. You are pieces of the person you're supposed to be.

What is IT?

Several dictionaries and online searches will define healing in the following ways;
- To become sound or healthy again
- To alleviate pain or illness
- To correct or put right

Healing is an action, a verb, something you have to DO. It is said that when something is unhealed, it exhibits a pattern that is unwanted. It's like the entire band is playing a Tupac song while the drummer is going full-fledged Rock n Roll playing a Chuck Berry song. The pattern and the beat are way off. To heal is to change the pattern. Healing is to experience the opposite. It is coming out of the darkness and being fully in the light. Healing is to be free from emotional incarceration, to be free to move. Healing is to drive down a road at 10 pm, but the sun is shining, and rain is pouring down, but not a drop is on your windshield so you can see clearly what is beyond you. Healing is, having the luxury of feeling.

In Dr. Thomas R. Egnews' article, *The Meaning of Healing: Transcending Suffering*, Healing was defined in terms of developing a sense of wholeness that involves physical, mental, emotional, social, and spiritual aspects of the human experience. In this article, the root of the word healing is also broken down deeper. "Heal" means "to make sound or whole again" and stems from the root, *haelan*, the condition or state of being *hal*, whole. *Hal* is also the root of "holy, defined as spiritually pure." You deserve to be whole.

Why haven't you begun the process of healing? Write down your reasons, your obstacles, your barriers, and your roadblocks.

Write it here or on a physical sheet of paper.
DO NOT TYPE IT on your phone.

_____

_____

_____

_____

_____

_____

Now that you have written them down, try and have an honest conversation with yourself and ask, are these reasons legitimate? If so, ask yourself, do you have the power to eliminate those reasons, those roadblocks? If the answer is yes, then why haven't you done it? If the answer is no, ask yourself, what or who is needed to assist me in doing so. Write down those answers too.

How Does Healing Work?

Healing is not one size fits all. The process of healing is different for every single person. What worked for her might not work for him. And because someone else's process might seem easier or harder, it is not to be compared to our own. Comparisons can lead to even more delay and denial of our healing journey.

Online, I saw a post that read, "To create my future, I had to revisit my past and revisit my pain." This is, in some cases, what healing is like. When I was in the 6th grade, I broke my right wrist while attempting to be LIKE MIKE, like most of the black boys around the world at the time. For the first few hours, I was in shock. What I was experiencing was almost unbelievable. I could literally see my bone poking up, trying to penetrate through my skin. Then it hit me, this was real, and I had no choice but to feel it. The pain was excruciating. I cried, wishing the pain would subside soon. I laid in the hospital bed with my mother beside me. The doctor placed my fingers in a device that held them tightly and suspended them in the air. He began the process that was necessary for my wrist to heal properly. It did not feel good. In fact, it hurt even more than the initial injury. This experience was a true example of *it getting worse before it gets better*. The doctor began to reset my bones. In other words, he had to do what felt like a deeper breaking of the bones. He grabbed my wrist where it hurt the most. I could literally hear the snapping and crackling of my bones. This had to be done to align the bones in a particular structure so that when the cast was placed over my wrist, the bones wouldn't begin to heal in some strange way.

It's just like when you have an open cut and your grandmother dashes alcohol over it. It stings badly. The wound has to be cleaned. You don't want a wound to start healing with all those impurities left lingering. I'm confident an infection would happen as a result. Then the next thing you know, what started off as a simple cut has now led to a whole limb being amputated. Now, you're walking around with an absent toe or finger all because you avoided the painful process of addressing your wound or, in this case, your struggle with mental illness. I know that was dramatic, but I think you get the point.

The treatment of wounds is often painful, unbearable even. But in order to heal properly, we must face that pain. There is no going over the problem, around the problem, or even under the problem. The only direction to go is THROUGH IT.

The Tools to Heal

Earlier, when defining mental health, I used an analogy that compares mental health to physical strength. How do you know when you're physically strong? When you are able to lift things that are considered heavy. How do you know when you're mentally healthy? When you are able to lift the heaviness of life's emotional, mental, or spiritual stressors. How do you know when you are not physically strong? When you are not able to lift heavy things. How do you know when you're not mentally healthy? I'd say when life's stressors are too heavy for you to lift or resolve. In these cases, what should we do? The answer is simple. When you are not able to lift a couch, it doesn't make you weak. It just means it's heavier than your norm, or maybe as a result of an illness, you have declined in your physical strength.

So, what do we do in these situations? We ask our neighbors or a friend to come help us move the couch. When you are mentally unhealthy, it simply means in that moment and time, you don't have the capacity to handle the heaviness of life's stressors as you normally would. You are not weak. You just need help moving the couch. It's time to get help, even if help is a tool or device of some sort. I recall using dolly plenty of times. If it's too heavy, then it's just too heavy. Do not break your back trying to lift something you are not capable of lifting on your own. And also, don't allow the heavy thing to sit there and fester like a sore because you're too stubborn, ashamed, embarrassed, or unsure of how to ask for help.

The definition of help is to make it easier (for someone) to do something by offering one's services or resources. Some synonyms for help are aid, assist, alleviate and make better. Help is a necessary tool we all need, especially in times when things are too heavy for us to carry alone. A tool is any instrument used to carry out a function. Not only are things like screwdrivers and drills tools, but people and even behaviors and activities can be too. What and who do you have in your toolbox? Let's take a look at some tools that have been known to help people heal.

Mental Health Therapy / Psychotherapy

Psychotherapy is the therapeutic treatment of mental illness provided by a trained mental health professional. Psychotherapy explores thoughts, feelings, and behaviors and seeks to improve an individual's well-being. Psychotherapy (sometimes) paired with medication is the most effective way to promote recovery. Examples include: Cognitive Behavioral Therapy, Exposure Therapy, Dialectical Behavior Therapy, etc.

Psychotherapy is the most common treatment for mental illness and mental health challenges such as depression, anxiety, emotional trauma, and more. It is important to note that therapy in any form does not work overnight, nor should it be expected to. I had stories of people quitting therapy after only one visit. The same way you can't go to the gym and lose 50 pounds after one workout, you also can't go to one therapy session and expect years of trauma to be healed or suddenly more manageable. IT IS A PROCESS. In my own journey, I almost found myself completely giving up on the idea of therapy because I felt unfairly judged and emotionally attacked by the therapist.

Overall, it just didn't feel like a safe space for me at that time. I later had to sit with that experience and ask myself, was this therapist not a good fit for me, or was I just not fit to handle the pressure or the work required to be successful in this scenario? Upon a deep reflection, I accepted that she just wasn't a good fit.

Finding a good therapist is very similar to finding a good significant other. You have to date around and collect some data. Sometimes you go on your first date, and they're perfect. The search is over. Other times, you have to keep dating for a while longer. Keep in mind that while in therapy, you are in a relationship, a deep and personal one too. In this relationship, there will be discomfort and growing pains. For the first time, you'll be challenged to look at things about yourself and others that you might not have considered before. But trust the process and give it time. Starting out, it may seem like a bunch of crooked paint strokes on a canvas. But in time, your therapist, much like an artist, will help you to see a very clear and colorful picture. Therapy works if you allow it to.

An easy way to find a therapist is to type it in your google search or go to www.PsychologyToday.com. When you get to this website, you can enter the type of issue you'd like to focus on, the gender or ethnicity of your desired therapist, and you can search to see what forms of payment they accept, such as health insurance, cash or employee assistance programs from your job. Therapy is a professional medical visit no different from an exam with your primary care physician, so your insurance will, in many cases, cover the expense.

Medication

Earlier, we discussed how in some cases, a mental illness could be more severe than others. In cases of more severity, medication is a viable option to assist in the healing process. Medication does not outrightly cure mental illness. However, according to *Mental Health America*, it may help with the management of symptoms. Medication paired with psychotherapy is the most effective way to promote recovery. In order to know if you need medication, you will first have to be diagnosed by a mental health professional who will, in turn, prescribe the necessary medications for your condition.

Hospitalization

According to *Mental Health America*, in a minority of cases, hospitalization may be necessary so that an individual can be closely monitored, accurately diagnosed, or have medications adjusted when his or her mental illness temporarily worsens.

Hospitalization can happen voluntarily or involuntarily. If you feel or think you will potentially cause harm to yourself or someone else, you can check yourself in at an emergency room or by contacting your primary care physician. This usually happens in cases of a crisis, such as suicide or substance use. Other cases dealing with schizophrenia, bipolar disorder, eating disorders, and many others have been the just cause for admission into a hospital. If you need help, I encourage you to go and get it. Do not overthink it. Your struggle is valid.

As a friend or family member of someone who may be experiencing an episode where they are a potential threat to their own safety or others, you too have the right to have them admitted. Sometimes, the person at risk could be in denial. This should be seen as a life-or-death situation. Your courage to identify their struggle and willingness to address it aggressively could be the very action that saves their life. They might not like you for it in the short run, but it is the long run that matters most.

Support Groups

A support group is a group meeting where members guide each other towards the shared goal of recovery. Support groups are often comprised of nonprofessionals and peers that have suffered from similar experiences.

Many might hear support groups and think of AA Meetings for Substance Abuse. TV and Film have done a great job at making us aware of support groups in this capacity. But, it's also necessary to know that there are support groups for so many other mental health challenges such as anxiety, grief, marriage, sexual assault, single mothers, recently freed from incarceration, and more. I even saw a support group for wives of preachers. That, I didn't expect to discover, but you never know who is in need of support or what resources exist specifically for people LIKE YOU until you search for them.

I never knew support groups for grief even existed until I

lost my mother and experienced the worst type of grief in my life. It was then I began seeking every life jacket in the sea because I was truly drowning by trying to swim alone, knowing how limp and weak I was in those moments.

How do you find support groups? You can simply type support groups in your google search or go to the PyschologyToday.com website. I personally learned about support groups from a counselor who helped me via the Crisis Text Line. I'll share more details on that resource below.

SELF CARE

In a *Right as Rain* article by UW Medicine, clinical social worker Morgan Turner explains, "self-care is the necessity to do things that are good for our physical, emotional or psychological well-being." In essence, it's doing something that helps your body, mind, or soul feel good. Take a moment and tell yourself, "I DESERVE GOOD THINGS!" And you truly do.

Self-care begins with loving yourself enough to show up for yourself. Self-care is listening to your emotions, mind, and body and catering to those needs. When your body communicates that it's tired, you ought to listen and rest. When your emotions communicate the need to express through shedding tears, take a break and cry it out. When your mind says to SAY NO, you should do it without hesitation. It would be a disservice to your own self to suppress your own needs and wants too.

What are some ways you can implement self-care into your life? I'd like to share a few, and then you can add more if you like.

- Soak in a hot bubble bath.
- Go get a manicure and pedicure.
- Get a full body massage.
- Meditate.
- Exercise! Go to the gym, do it at home or walk the neighborhood.
- Eat healthy food.
- Rest, BE STILL.

- Sleep in.

- Buy yourself a meaningful gift.

- Say NO to what doesn't FEEL GOOD to you.

- Turn off your phone for 1 to 2 hours or a full day.

- Fast from social media.

- Relax by a body of water.

- Journaling

- Doing absolutely NOTHING!

- Listening to comedy and laughing out loud.

- Cuddle with your pet.

- Hang with friends or family who make you happy.

SELF CARE

Take care of yourself,
it's important!

TYPES OF SELF-CARE

PHYSICAL
Sleep
Stretching
Walking
Physical release
Healthy food
Yoga
Rest

EMOTIONAL
Stress managment
Emotional maturity
Forgiveness
Compassion
Kindness

SOCIAL
Boundaries
Support systems
Positive social media
Communication
Time together
Ask for help

SPIRITUAL
Time alone
Meditation
Yoga
Connection
Nature
Journaling
Sacred space

PERSONAL
Hobbies
Knowing yourself
Personal identity
Honoring your true self

SPACE
Safety
Healthy living environment
Security and stability
Organized space

FINANCIAL
Saving
Budgeting
Money management
Splurging
Paying bills

WORK
Time management
Work boundaries
Positive workplace
More learning
Break time

SELF-CARE REMINDER CARDS

CLEANSE YOUR BODY   INSPIRE YOUR MIND

PAMPER YOURSELF   CREATE YOUR SPACE

NOURISH YOUR BODY   CONNECT WITH OTHERS

SELF-CARE REMINDER CARDS

PLAY - HAVE FUN   GO OUTDOORS

TREAT YOURSELF   RELAX - CHILL

STAY HYDRATED   DRESS COMFORTABLY

Self-Care Goals

PHYSICAL

EMOTIONAL

SPIRITUAL

INTELLECTUAL

SOCIAL

ENVIRONMENTAL

SELF-CARE NOTES

Self-Care Journal

Today, I struggled with.....

I got through the struggle by....

Ways I loved on myself today.....

Tomorrow, I will not give my energy to......

Today, I stopped and noticed.....

Resources from Your Phone-

Suicide & Crisis Lifeline

You can simply dial 988 or send a text message. Real-life professional counselors will take your call and speak with you about your crisis within minutes. When in a crisis, I would encourage you to call the number immediately. They will even connect you to free therapy options in your city and state. For more information, visit www.988lifeline.org

Crisis Text Line

This is a very valuable resource if you desire a very low-impact interaction with a trained counselor. You can simply text 741741. They will respond by asking permission to connect you with a crisis counselor, and within minutes, you will have someone to aid you through your crisis. I personally used this text line while grieving, and it helped tremendously. My counselor made me aware of grief support groups in my area and virtual options. I had never even heard of support groups for grief before our communication. If you need this resource, use it. It helps.

CHAPTER 4

THE LANGUAGE & EMOTIONAL LITERACY

An emotion is a spontaneous mental reaction, such as joy, sorrow, hate, and love. Emotions always involve mental activity and sometimes have physical effects on the body.

Can you read emotions? Can you read your own emotions or others? Have you ever experienced a particular emotion expressed by someone or even by yourself, and you didn't understand what it meant? If the answer is YES, you might be emotionally illiterate. This is common, so don't worry. We can begin changing that today.

Many people are emotionally illiterate because they can't read or comprehend emotions. How do you learn to read literature? You first have to learn the alphabet, then the sounds of each letter, and next, how to connect the sounds to form words. To become a reader who comprehends the information, you must understand the definition of the words. It's not enough to just be able to read the word. You must also be able to define the word. Once you're able to define the word, you must also learn tone and context.

When I think about context, I think of the adage, "read between the lines." There is a unique science to learning to read literature. To my point, learning to read emotions isn't much different. But it also doesn't have to be a complicated process.

I, for one, have found myself completely missing the bus several times. I recall one instance in particular in the summer of 2021, my niece and my daughters asked me throughout the day to take them to the skating rink. After they asked me 39 million times, I finally obliged. So, we got to the skating rink that evening, and everyone ran to the line excited. Well, everyone except for my niece. She instead sat by the door with her arms crossed and hesitating to come in. I went over to check on her, and to my surprise, she didn't want to go in at all. She asked if she could go home instead because she wasn't comfortable with so many people there. She even became emotionally charged. Immediately I was confused. After trying to encourage her a few times to go in, I grew frustrated. I had concluded that she was "JUST BEING A BRAT." It wasn't until a year later, after I finished my certification for Mental Health First Aid, that I realized my niece was actually experiencing a full-blown anxiety attack. It was recently that I apologized to her for misreading her emotional experience and handling her with so little care due to my ignorance, my emotional illiteracy, and emotional unintelligence.

How many times have you missed the bus? How many times have you mistaken someone's emotional episode for something completely opposite from what it was? How has that impacted your relationships? Let's flip it. How would you feel if someone misread your emotions? Has it happened before? If so, how did it make you feel? How many times have you mistaken your own emotional episodes for something completely opposite from what it was? As a black man, I've often expressed anger, but truly it was disappointment or sadness that I was feeling. But because I lacked the language, the understanding, and the literacy to properly read emotions, I often found myself identifying all my emotional episodes as the one emotion I was mostly allowed to and conditioned to experience due to my societal norms, anger. It's like going to a doctor for a broken leg, but he keeps treating you for a broken arm because all he's ever learned to understand is a broken arm.

That is probably not the best doctor to see unless you have broken arms, of course. But this is how many of us are doctoring our own emotions and the emotions of the people we are in relationships with. We skate around the core of the issues because it's the easiest thing to do, especially when you don't know how to engage properly with something.

It's like when a person who only speaks English is trying to have a conversation with a person who only speaks Spanish. Both people are looking at each other with their eyes squinted, using body gestures with their hands, and raising and lowering their voices as they struggle to communicate and sift through language barriers. They are both confused and frustrated. Eventually, one of the two gives up or just assumes that they know what is being said and offer a response that is insufficient or not at all in alignment with what the other person was asking for. This, too, happens with us and our emotions. When your thoughts emote, the emotions are actually trying to communicate something to you. I know personally, I've been in situations where my emotions were speaking loudly to me, but I had no clear idea what they were saying, so I ran with what I thought I knew.

If I'm being transparent, I didn't know the language well enough to hear what my own emotions were trying to communicate to me. I thought the emotion was telling me to be angry and fight, but it was really saying, "BE STILL, REMOVE YOURSELF FROM THE SPACE, CHANGE

ENVIRONMENT." I thought the emotion was saying,
"Your dad doesn't love you, and you should hate him, be
angry," but it was really saying, "You are disappointed, and
you should seek to understand his position."

Emotions are communicators to your entire body and mind.
So, listen to them and address them soon. If your emotions
are ignored for too long or misheard, they will react. It is

not healthy to put emotions away in a box just because you don't understand them right away or because they trigger discomfort. If you put them away in one box, they will, one day, without warning, pop out of another box that you cannot control. Emotions, if not tended to properly, can literally paralyze you mentally and physically too.

It's not only necessary to understand the language of emotions from the standpoint of what they are saying. It is also necessary to know the language of emotions on a rudimentary level. I spoke to this earlier when defining the process of reading. It's great to be able to sound out the word, but you must also be able to define what those words even mean so you can comprehend the actual text. It is nearly impossible to begin healing if you can't so much as identify what the emotion is that you're experiencing and how to define it. You must have the language to call it out. When you don't, it's a lot like being muted or being stuck in a box, and the only way you can be saved is if you say correctly what it is that has you trapped. Let's get closer to being free right now. Let's define the emotions and get one step closer to mastering the language.

"In 1980, the Emotion Wheel was created by psychologist Robert Pletcher to help organize complex emotions and so that people could more easily gain clarity, identify, and label their emotions. Given the complexity of emotions, Robert Plutchik created the Emotion Wheel to visualize the complexity of emotions and help people identify and label their emotions. The Emotion Wheel uses color to depict discrete emotions and blends of emotion, uses their gradients to express intensity, and uses the geometric shape to reflect the polarity (or similarity) of emotions.

Plutchik believed that there are eight primary emotions, represented by primary colors, that vary in intensity. The middle of the emotion wheel reflects the maximal levels of arousal of each emotion:

Grief

Loathing

Terror

Vigilance

Rage

Admiration

Amusement

Ecstasy

The emotions further away from the center of the emotion wheel represent milder arousal levels of the primary emotions. Emotions placed closer to each other in the emotion wheel are deemed more similar than those farther apart. The words outside of the "slices" in the emotion wheel are common blends of emotion (e.g., "surprise" and "sadness" combine to produce "disapproval").

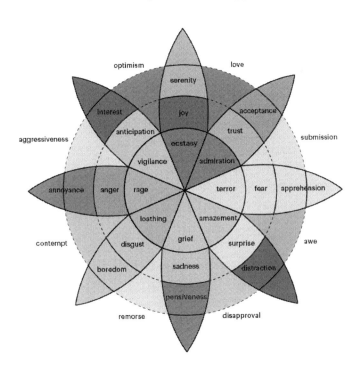

Plutchik argued that each emotion serves an evolutionary function. He identified the following survival behaviors as triggered by each emotion:

Subjective	Behavior	Function
Fear	Withdrawing	Protection
Anger	Attacking	Destruction
Joy	Mating	Reproduction
Sadness	Crying for help	Reintegration
Acceptance, Trust	Pair bonding	Incorporation
Disgust	Vomiting	Rejection
Expectancy	Examining	Exploration
Surprise	Freezing	Orientation

For example, feelings of fear/terror result in withdrawing behaviors that are meant to protect oneself. In our ancestors, fear or terror may have been caused by seeing a wild animal and running away in order to preserve their life. In current times, fear or terror can result from psychological threats of rejection, which can lead some people to run away in order to keep themselves from getting hurt" (Karnilowicz, N.D.).

EMOTIONS VOCABULARY

Grief - intense emotional suffering caused by loss, disaster, misfortune, etc.; acute sorrow; deep sadness.

Loathing - strong dislike or disgust; intense aversion.

Terror - a state of intense or overwhelming fear.

Vigilance - state of alertness in which an appropriate response is made to a stimulus.

Rage - violent and uncontrolled anger.

Admiration - a feeling of respect and approval.

Ecstasy - a state of extreme happiness, especially when feeling pleasure.

Amazement - overwhelming surprise or astonishment.

Anticipation - a feeling of excitement about something that is going to happen in the near future.

Anger - human emotion that involves intense displeasure and aggression as a response to an aggravating event. A strong feeling of displeasure and belligerence aroused by a wrong, wrath; ire.

Disgust - a strong feeling of disapproval and dislike at a situation, a person's behavior, etc.

Sadness - the feeling of being unhappy, especially because something bad has happened.

Surprise - the feeling caused by something unexpected happening.

Fear - a distressing emotion aroused by impending danger, evil, pain, etc., whether the threat is real or imagined; the feeling or condition of being afraid.

Trust - confident expectation of something; hope. Reliance on and confidence in the truth, worth, reliability, etc., of a person or thing; faith.

Joy - the emotion of great delight or happiness caused by something exceptionally good or satisfying; keen pleasure; elation.

Interest - the sense of curiosity about or concern with something or someone.

Serenity - peaceful and calm.

Acceptance - favorable reception; approval; favor.

Apprehension - an anticipation of adversity or misfortune; suspicion or fear of future trouble or evil.

Distraction - an interruption; an obstacle to concentration.

Pensiveness - deeply or seriously thoughtful, often with a tinge of sadness.

Boredom - the feeling of being wearied by dullness, tedious repetition, etc.

Annoyance – an unpleasant mental state that is characterized by irritation and distraction from one's conscious thinking. It can lead to emotions such as frustration and anger.

Aggressiveness - vigorously energetic, esp. in the use of initiative and forcefulness.
Boldly assertive and forward; pushy.

Contempt - the attitude or feeling of a person towards a person or thing that he considers worthless or despicable; scorn.

Remorse – a feeling of sadness and being sorry for something you have done.

Disapproval – the expression or feeling that something done or said is wrong.

Awe – a feeling of great respect sometimes mixed with fear or surprise.

Submission – Surrendering power to something or someone; obedient. Yielding to the control, authority, or choice of another.

Love - an intense emotion of affection, warmth, fondness, and regard towards a person or thing.

Optimism - the tendency to expect the best and see the best in all things; hopefulness and confidence.

<u>More Emotions to Understand</u>

Disappointment - the unhappiness or discouragement that results when your hopes or expectations have not been satisfied, or someone or something is not as good as you had hoped or expected.

Jealousy - a feeling of unhappiness and anger because

someone has something or someone that you want.

Amusement - a feeling of being entertained and happy.

Obsession - the domination of one's thoughts or feelings by a persistent idea, image, desire, etc.

Congratulations, you did it! Let's take a moment to pause and make a note of what just happened here. You just did some good work. You took time to learn the language and literacy around mental health and emotions. This is a huge step towards the work necessary for healing. But don't just read this once. Come back to these definitions often, especially when you are emotionally charged or if someone else is.

Use this word bank as a resource of understanding. It's too risky to assume what the emotion is. Even when you get to a place where you feel you're a master of understanding emotions, still come back here every now and again for a refresher. Emotions, as you just read, can be complex. They have ranges and levels. Some emotions are a combination of multiple emotions. Use the Emotion Wheel to see how some of the emotions connect, intersect and parallel with one another.

Also, some other emotions that are not mentioned here may come up for you. I encourage you to do some leg work and define them. Write them down in a journal, and keep a log of the vocabulary you learn. Understanding emotions and what they are communicating might be the very tool that saves your life or someone else's. So, take it seriously.

CHAPTER 5

HEALTHY HABITS

Welcome to yet another step towards your healing journey. So far, many valuable topics have been covered. I hope that you have been able to grab some useful tools and resources to help you towards getting off the couch. If it counts for anything, I'd like to say I BELIEVE YOU ARE GETTING CLOSER. If you're taking the time to read this, you must desire to be in a better space. That alone deserves praise. You are making progress.

I will say this several times, so we don't forget. Healing is indeed a *journey*, not a destination. It is a road you will always be traveling on. Even after you have arrived at a brighter place, work will always be required to maintain the light in your life. This is why while on our journey, we should develop healthy habits. A habit is a recurrent, often unconscious, pattern of behavior that is acquired through frequent repetition. Some simple habits many of us have in common are things such as brushing our teeth in the morning, using the restroom and putting down the toilet seat. Some other habits might be checking your phone when you wake up, using certain phrases every time you speak, or ordering the same food daily. A lot of times, we don't even notice certain things are habits until someone points them out to us. Every time I'm in a conversation, I use the phrase, "Well, the point is" or "What are you even talking about." I didn't notice until my significant other started joking about it one day, and we laughed together about it once I realized I do say those things A LOT.

What are some of your habits? How did those habits come about? Maybe you saw your father or mother doing it every day as a kid, and you just picked up the behavior too. Maybe your favorite music artist did it, and you subconsciously followed suit. My girlfriend breaks into this annoying B. Simone voice every time she gets excited and doesn't even realize it until I say it to her. (By the way, I don't think B. Simone is annoying, she's hilarious!)

Are your habits healthy? Are they good for you? If smoking a cigarette is something you do after every meal then it's a habit, but honestly, is it good for you? Do the habits you partake in make your life better? Bad habits; we have to begin breaking them before they break us. I once had a friend who lied like it was normal. He did it so much that he genuinely didn't know when he was doing it most of the time. And he was honestly a good person. But it was a habit that he unfortunately adopted. Our friend group eventually just accepted him as a liar, always participated in conversations with him with much caution, and never really believed him, even if he was actually telling the truth this time. This was no good for him or us. Eventually, I had to sit him down and have a true intervention. He's gotten a lot better since then, but it wasn't easy.

Take some time right now to write down some habits you may have that are NOT SO GOOD. A way to determine if they aren't good is by analyzing the past and making notes if the habits have caused turmoil in a relationship, caused you to lose something or someone, or in some small or major way affected you emotionally, mentally, spiritually, or physically. Better yet, if you keep up with this habit, can it eventually cause some level of harm more than it does good?

_____

_____

_____

_____

_____

Now that you've identified some of those bad habits lets begin breaking them. And no, it won't happen overnight. Don't expect it to be easy. It's work. It requires you to be assertive towards your own self and in your relationships with others sometimes. I decided I wanted to break the habit of drinking alcohol, so I created a tangible goal. I'd only drink on Saturday or Sunday each week. Even then, my limit is two drinks max. I even avoided going out with certain friends during the week because I knew they would buy me free drinks and encourage the behavior. After sticking to this routine for a while, it was long before I was able to manage going out and not drinking at all.

It takes 21 days to develop or break a habit. I offer to you this mantra;

Do it small.

Do it for 21 minutes every day for 21 days.

While doing the work to break bad habits, also be developing new habits that are healthy. When considering the new habits you desire to include in your life, think of things that deserve to be in your life EVERY DAY. Those things should consist of things that make you happy and keep you balanced and healthy.

Allow healthy habits to become your new distractions from the old bad habits. You might think of smoking a cigarette, but instead, do 40 push-ups or go for a walk. Put the healthy habits you are developing on the calendar with an alert or a reminder daily, so it never leaves your consciousness. Eventually, it will become an unconscious behavior, and now you're locked in, focused, and on your way to a healthier lifestyle.

CHAPTER 6

LET'S WRITE ABOUT IT

This is probably my favorite part of the book. Why? Because I am a nerd when it comes to writing. For the last decade, I've been a professional spoken word artist. I've been in love with writing even longer. Having poetry writing as a tool has by far been one of the most significant resources in my life that have helped me navigate my mental health struggles. Since 7th grade in Ms. Murphy's science class, I've used poetry as my voice and my way to express my innermost feelings and thoughts. I recall even way back then being comfortable, through my poetry, of course, to express that I was sad, angry, or in love. I still have the poems and love letters to prove it. Writing gave me a license to dig deeper than the average child back then. I was so in tune with who I was. I think it had a lot to do with me feeling safe within the borders of my notebook pages. I poured it all out.

In this portion of the book, I am going to encourage you to do the same. I am the founder and director of an organization known as Creative Connections. I am very active with my organization as a teaching artist. As a teaching artist, I go into schools and classrooms around the country with the purpose of integrating creative writing, mostly poetry, into the classroom. While in such settings with students and oftentimes with educators for professional development, my focus is always social-emotional learning. I encourage my participants to think about the following; How do you feel? Why do you feel it? And how do we go about healing from it, or if the emotion is good, how do we maintain it?

Right now, let's do it. Let's write about it. Grab a piece of paper, not a phone, either. I want you to be connected to the words you write. We spend more than enough time on our phones and operating our technology as is. For this exercise, disconnect from those things, and let's connect with self. The goal is to express how we feel or something we've felt before.

What's something you've experienced that you've never had an opportunity to talk about or heal from? Is there a time you've been extremely sad, angry, disappointed, frustrated, or deeply confused? I'd like you to pinpoint that emotion, that day and time, the scenario as you best recall, and let's write. Follow the steps below as you write your very own poem.

One thing to know, a poem has no rules. Just write it and mean it. That is enough. Everything else is extra icing on the cake. Below I will offer some icing on the cake. Insert celebration emoji and praise hands because WE LIT!

1. Write a haiku about the emotion you are experiencing now or in the past. A haiku is a short Japanese poem. It is written in three lines with a total of 17 syllables. The

first line should be five syllables, the second line should be seven syllables, and the third line should be five syllables.

Haiku Example:

I am not okay.

I feel robbed of all my joy.

I am drowning here.

2. Write five sentences using the five senses to express yourself. This will help us to begin better painting pictures with our words.

5 Senses Example:

It felt like I was drowning in a pool of tears.

I could see death above the water dressed in all black.

He smelt like a familiar odor, disgusting and dirty.

I could hear my mother telling me to swim.

It was then I remembered the sweet, savory taste of life.

3. Now, let's write a simile. A simile is a figurative language where two unlike things, are compared using

LIKE or AS. Be sure to identify the two things being compared and the use of the connecting word, which will always be LIKE or AS.

Simile Examples:

The <u>tears</u> on my face felt <u>like</u> <u>waterfalls</u> that wouldn't stop running.

Her <u>words</u> were heavy <u>as</u> a bag of <u>bricks</u> in the arms of a toddler.

4. Personification is my favorite figurative language skill. In this one, you simply use your imagination and give a non-living thing human characteristic.

Personification Examples:

The depression held me hostage in my bed, and I felt I couldn't escape.

Happiness swept me off my feet and carried me to a soft place.

His words slapped me in the face and yanked my heart clean from my chest.

So now that you've done these exercises, let's go to a clean sheet of paper and put all these skills to use. The goal is still to express yourself. Say how you feel. Don't hold anything in or back. This exercise is only effective when the truth is evident. Let's raise the stakes even more. Your poem should be at least one full page. I am sure you have a lot to say. If one page is easy, go for two pages.

Read your poem aloud to yourself several times. It's important to hear yourself aloud, even if it's a little awkward at first. Lastly, once you've heard enough, grab a friend or someone you trust and ask them to JUST LISTEN to your poem. If you do not desire any feedback, let them know this ahead of time.

I am so excited about your poems. And, of course, I'd love to hear them or read them. My email is always open. If you're feeling really bold and ready to share your truth, post your poem on social media and encourage others that it's okay to express themselves and tell their story. Don't forget to tag me too. @ChrisJamesJourney

CHAPTER 7

WHAT IS HAPPINESS & HOW DO I GET IT?

When people ask me how I am doing, my response 90 percent of the time is, "I'm happy." And maybe 85 percent of the time, I actually mean it. We all know what happiness is, and I'd say with confidence that we've all experienced it at one time or another in our lives. It felt good, didn't it? You felt a sense of warmth all over your body. You smiled, laughed probably. You felt light, not heavy, and you yourself were light even when darkness was around you. Happiness delivered to you, satisfaction and pleasure emotionally, mentally, physically, and spiritually.

The last time you were happy, what was the cause of it? I

want you to pause right now and really think. Again, this is an interactive book, so if you will, please make note of those moments, those thoughts that gave birth to your happiness. Think of those thoughts as art and hang them on the walls of your mind. What happens to your body when happiness occurs? You smile, laugh, blush, dance, celebrate, cry sometimes, and take deep breaths of relief.

Are you happy right now? If so, why? If you're not happy, why aren't you? Were you happy today, and something happened that caused your mood to change? The thing that happened, did you have control of it? Is it at all even possible to alter time and change the occurrence that affected your mood? I'd answer NO. Does it serve you in any positive way to allow that occurrence to hold a position of power over your mood? Does that occurrence actually have power? If so, how did it gain power? Who controls if it maintains power over your mood? If it's living in your mind, rent-free at that, who is really in control? YOU ARE!

One might argue that happiness is always fleeting, that it comes and goes. I'd argue that those same people have attached happiness to actual things, opportunities, and even people, which in actuality are always fleeting. So, when these things aren't present, they have convinced themselves that happiness cannot be either. I disagree wholeheartedly. When your bank account is low or your love life is non-existent, happiness can still be fully available to you.

Happiness, like all emotions, begins in the mind. So, is it true that happiness lives in the mind? Can we think happy thoughts enough, and it becomes our reality? If you think negative thoughts enough, you can surely be consumed by negative emotions; that I know for sure. So, if you think and spend time with happy thoughts enough then I am sure that positive emotions will consume your mind. I think it is almost impossible to think about memories that felt good and laughter that made you break into tears of joy and, in turn, have a frown on your face.

Epictetus teaches in the book *The Art of Mastering Life* that we should learn to distinguish what we can and cannot control. Within our control are our own opinions, aspirations, desires, and the things that repel us. Happiness is threatened when we allow our happiness to be connected to external conditions that are beyond our control. We cannot control other people. We cannot control whether opportunities will continue flowing in or not. We cannot control if someone rushing on the road crashes into our car that we can't afford to get repaired. And I'm sure we all know that we absolutely cannot control the weather. But we do have control over how we respond to all these occurrences. The power, the control, and the mastery of happiness are truly in your own mind.

When I think of happiness, I think of success. For me, to have success is to have three things; peace, balance, and freedom. If any of the three are missing from your equation, success is not completely present. I feel the same way about happiness. When you have it, you should also have peace, balance, and freedom.

Peace and happiness go hand in hand. When you have happiness in your life, peace should be the shield that safeguards it for you. Peace is defined as calm and quiet; freedom from worry or annoyance. Although peace can be considered a soft place, it can also be a powerful weapon to use in your defense, especially when forces beyond your control attempt to rob you of your happiness or your sanity. Peace is a RADICAL practice, and your mind must be trained to acquire it and maintain it.

Before you can command peace around you, you must command peace within you. So BE STILL and allow the storm to rage. The chaos of the world, the distractions that have the ability to disturb you emotionally, mentally, spiritually, and physically will always creep outside the doorsteps and windows of your mind. Sometimes, those distractions will actually find their way into your mind, but when weaponized with peace, you can surely have them vacate the premises of your mind before they have the opportunity to fester and infect your mood long-term.

In 1985, Rupert Hitzig and Berry Gordy produced the first American martial arts film that starred an all-black cast. In the film, a character infamously known as Sho'Nuff went around Harlem on a mission to prove that he was the baddest fighter the city had ever seen. He was loud, rough around the edges, and could fight really well. But a young man affectionately known as Bruce Leeroy was actually the best fighter in the city. Unlike his antagonist, he had no desire to prove it. Every time Sho'Nuff ran into Bruce Leeroy, he would try everything to get Bruce Leeroy to fight him. He'd yell, make threats, and even throw dozens of wild punches barely missing Leeroy's face. But Leeroy always stood there calm, silent, unbothered. Leeroy was weaponized with true peace so much that the encounter of actual danger didn't cause him to react in panic or for his mood to change. He was always able to access the situation in a way that he maintained control of the situation and of his emotions. This is why Bruce Leeroy Green was the best fighter and possessed THE GLOW.

Peace will make you the best fighter in your life. Peace belongs to you. You should claim it. Remember, peace is a radical practice. It is serious business. Practice acquiring it daily, and eventually, it will always be yours, and you can rest assured that happiness will follow.

CHAPTER 8

HOW TO BE A FRIEND?

Being a friend is not a title that should be taken lightly. Oftentimes as a friend, you are closer to a person than their blood relatives by choice, and by default, you become their first line of defense and comfort. If someone is deemed a friend, this means they are highly trusted with your emotions, energy, thoughts, and dreams. As a friend, you have access to very valuable assets of another human being. You should guard those assets as though they are fragile artifacts.

In this short chapter, I am here to focus on one area we should show up in as friends, and that is mental health. The worst thing you can do is be a friend of someone who is experiencing serious mental health struggles and do nothing as they decline.

In May of 2022, I became certified in Mental Health First Aid by the *National Council for Well-Being*. I encourage every single person reading this to go get certified. I invested eight hours, and I believe that it has truly transformed how I show up in relationships, in my work, and in my overall life in the greatest of ways. I could've gotten certified in CPR so I could save the next person struggling to breathe, which has been a really rare occurrence in my life. I instead got certified in Mental Health First Aid because I can't recall one day when I got on social media, went to a store, or worked out at the gym, and I didn't see a person struggling to hold on to their mental health. When someone is dealing with a mental health struggle or crisis, Mental Health First Aid provides a MENTAL HEALTH ACTION PLAN using the acronym

A.L.G.E.E:

Assess for risk of suicide or harm

Listen non-judgmentally

Give reassurance and information

Encourage appropriate professional help

Encourage self-help and other strategies

HOW TO APPROACH

Not Helpful Approaches

1. I can understand and know exactly what you are going through. The same thing happened to me two years ago.
2. You'll get over it. You should just ignore it and get on with life.
3. Pull yourself together.
4. It's such a beautiful day outside. How can you feel so sad?
5. You'll feel better tomorrow.
6. I'd like to stop and talk, but I've got to go. I'll give you a call later.
7. You're here to work and have a job to do. It is time ot get on with it.

Helpful Approaches

1. Have you talked to anyone about this before?
2. How long have you been feeling like this?
3. I am really concerned about you.
4. Is something bothering you?
5. You haven't been hanging with us lately. Is everything okay?
6. I don't understand exactly what you are going through but I can see that it is affecting for you.
7. Let's go and have a cup of tea.
8. Something seems to be bothering you. Do you want to talk about it?

Sometimes, the mental health challenge your friend is facing might not be as severe as suicide ideation but still, cause enough attention. As friends, it's easy to get caught up in these false narratives such as "That doesn't have anything to do with me" or "If they are dealing with something, I'm sure they'd say something about it." And we end up just being bystanders instead of asserting ourselves. How can we go about asserting ourselves in a way that is healthy?

A - ASK questions, do not assume

S - STUDY the behaviors and the language of your friends, so you best assess their emotional and mental temperature. Be a STUDENT in their situation.

S - be SOLUTION based; how can I help? Don't offer a solution that you believe to be the absolute and THE way.

E - ENGAGE with your friend thoroughly. Do not break eye contact or allow phone calls or other activities to distract you from paying full attention.

R - <u>R</u>ECOGNIZE that their emotional episode is not about you, so remove your personal guilt or opinions.

T - <u>T</u>rust their <u>T</u>RUTH. It is not the appropriate time to debate their experience or to overly intellectualize their feelings and thoughts. It is not for you to fully understand or agree with.

"We have two ears and one mouth so that we can listen twice as much as we speak" (Epictetus, N.D.). This is some of the best advice I've ever received. I have learned to listen not only with my ears but with my eyes, my heart, and my intuition. It is often what my friends aren't saying from their mouths that they need me to hear the most. All scars and illnesses aren't visible to the eye.

Being a friend is an important role. You are needed in all ways. Don't ever underestimate your value and significance in a person's life. Stay close to your friends. Be in tune with their patterns, and if at any moment they are off-beat, do not hesitate or wait for permission to be given before you ASSERT yourself. Their healing might depend on you.

THE OUTRO

GET UP, GET OUT & GET SOME HEALING

Somebody cues the beat. Turn my mic up some. Alright, so boom. You made it to the final track. You made it to "an ending." Notice that I didn't say, "THE ENDING." I say that because the journey has only begun. You still have so much further to go, so much more to do. I hope that as a result of reading this book, you gained something, whether it was new information, affirmations, or reminders you needed.

It was my goal to break down the process of healing in a very practical way. I hope I accomplished that. I hope that you are inspired, fired up, and ready to do the work to get off the couch. Healing is probably the most self-fulfilling work you can ever do. There is no reward in avoiding healing, but it is everything and more to accept the journey. Get up, lose the weight, forgive those who contributed hurt to your heart, forgive yourself, start over and accept what once was, is no more. Doing this only propels you higher. Forgiveness is for you. Holding on to things that no longer serve you holds you, hostage, so get free. Losing that weight is going to contribute to you potentially living longer, being happier, and loving yourself even more.

Stop running away from what is good for you. You deserve good things. And the best thing you can afford yourself is a healthy life.

And if by now you happen to already be off the couch, I pray that you feel inclined to help someone else get up. After all, a helping hand is what we all want and need. In our struggles, we desperately wish for someone to just see us, hear us, and assure us that better days are near. Be that for someone else. You, of all people, know how valuable it is to have a lifeline.

As we depart ways, for now, know that healing is like a book. If you start with a word, it leads to a sentence. When you have a sentence, it can lead to a paragraph. Once you have a paragraph, you can begin writing a story.

Healing is a one-step, at a time type of journey. It is to be done at your own pace. There is no right way to do it, just more effective steps you can take. So, whatever happens, just keep writing, keep living, and eventually, your healing story will be a best-selling novel. The world around you will be a much brighter place because you made the choice to push up from sinking in between the cushions, stretched your legs, and did the work to get off the couch and HEAL.

LET THE HEALING BEGIN...

ABOUT THE AUTHOR

Chris James is a man who is truly on a journey to impact and changes lives in his community and the world. Chris James is a national award-winning spoken word poet, TED Talk speaker, playwright, educator, screenwriter, and published author.

As a screenwriter, Chris most recently wrote the film
DEVON'S DAY, which premiered June 19, 2022, on BET
Networks.

In June 2019, he was the keynote speaker at the United
States Capitol for the 39th Annual Congressional Arts
Competition. Also, in 2019, his stage play Dear Black
People won Best Original play at the Atlanta Black Theatre
Festival. He is the author of Joe Got Flow, Black Boy
Blues, and The Odds Against US. In 2018, Arkansas PBS
filmed a short documentary about the life of Chris
James. In 2016, he was featured on the front cover of
Arkansas Times Newspaper for being one of Arkansas' top
visionaries.

Chris is a member of the Foreign Tongues poetry slam
team, which ranked 2nd place in the world's second-largest
poetry competition in 2014. He is the founder of Arkansas'
only poetry venue and second black-owned gallery, The
House of Art. As a teaching artist, Chris develops and
facilitates art-integrated poetry writing and performance
workshops for K-12 across the country. Through his work,

he educates on racial barriers and socio-economic challenges and how we can overcome them. As a certified Mental Health First Aider, he spearheads two programs, *The Fellas Mixer* and *Black Boys Better*, that focus on healing and growing black males in Atlanta, Georgia.

LET'S GET CONNECTED!

GET OFF THE COUCH is a touring community-based workshop and conversation facilitated by Chris James and other mental health advocates. This program is a true experience designed to inspire actions and results. We would love the opportunity to visit your city.

Get in touch by visiting

www.GetOfftheCouch.Live

or

www.TheChrisJamesJourney.com

WHO HELPED WITH THIS BOOK

Illustrations Provided By

LeRon McAdoo, Visual Contributor

www.BackYardOnline.com

Editing Provided By

Doris Foster

https://www.fiverr.com/doris_foster

Resource Guide

Chapter 1

Homepage - National Council for Mental Wellbeing (thenationalcouncil.org)

MentalHealth.Gov

Chapter 2

Microaggressions: Definition, types, and examples (medicalnewstoday.com)

GeneralMHFacts (nami.org)

Conditions and treatments - Better Health Channel

https://www.betterhealth.vic.gov.au/health/servicesandsupport/types-of-mental-health-issues-and-illnesses

Chapter 3

Egnew TR. The meaning of healing: transcending suffering. Ann Fam Med. 2005 May-Jun;3(3):255-62. doi: 10.1370/afm.313. PMID: 15928230; PMCID: PMC1466870 255egnew.indd (nih.gov)

www.MentalHealthAmerica.org

www.PsychologyToday.com

Crisis Text Line | Text HOME To 741741 free, 24/7 Crisis Counseling

https://rightasrain.uwmedicine.org/mind/mental-health/self-care-meaning

www.988lifeline.org

Chapter 4

https://www.dictionary.com/browse/emotion

Mental Health First Aid

Asad Ali Shah S, Yezhuang T, Muhammad Shah A, Khan Durrani D, Jamal Shah S. Fear of Terror and Psychological Well-Being: The Moderating Role of Emotional Intelligence. Int J Environ Res Public Health. 2018 Nov 14;15(11):2554. doi: 10.3390/ijerph15112554. PMID: 30441857; PMCID: PMC6267429. Fear of Terror and Psychological Well-Being: The Moderating Role of Emotional Intelligence (nih.gov)

https://www.berkeleywellbeing.com/emotion-wheel.html

https://www.collinsdictionary.com/dictionary/english/grief

https://www.dictionary.com/browse/loathing

https://www.merriam-webster.com/dictionary/terror

https://www.sciencedirect.com/topics/neuroscience/
vigilance

https://www.merriam-webster.com/dictionary/rage

https://www.merriam-webster.com/dictionary/admiration

https://dictionary.cambridge.org/us/dictionary/english/
ecstasy

https://www.collinsdictionary.com/us/dictionary/english/
amazement

https://dictionary.cambridge.org/us/dictionary/english/
anticipation

https://www.dictionary.com/browse/anger

https://dictionary.cambridge.org/us/dictionary/english/
disgust

https://dictionary.cambridge.org/us/dictionary/english/
sadness

https://dictionary.cambridge.org/us/dictionary/english/
surprise

https://www.dictionary.com/browse/fear

https://www.dictionary.com/browse/trust

https://www.dictionary.com/browse/joy

https://www.dictionary.com/browse/interest

https://dictionary.cambridge.org/us/dictionary/english/serenity

https://www.dictionary.com/browse/acceptance

https://www.dictionary.com/browse/apprehension

https://www.dictionary.com/browse/distraction

https://www.dictionary.com/browse/pensiveness

https://www.dictionary.com/browse/boredom

https://en.wikipedia.org/wiki/Annoyance

https://www.collinsdictionary.com/us/dictionary/english/aggressive
https://www.dictionary.com/browse/contempt

https://dictionary.cambridge.org/us/dictionary/english/remorse

https://dictionary.cambridge.org/us/dictionary/english/disapproval

https://dictionary.cambridge.org/us/dictionary/english/awe

https://www.dictionary.com/browse/love

https://www.dictionary.com/browse/optimism

https://dictionary.cambridge.org/us/dictionary/english/disappointment

https://dictionary.cambridge.org/us/dictionary/english/jealousy

https://www.vocabulary.com/dictionary/amusement

https://www.dictionary.com/browse/obsession

Chapter 5

https://www.dictionary.com/browse/habit

Chapter 6

Haiku Definition & Meaning | Dictionary.com

Simile Definition & Meaning | Dictionary.com

Personification Definition & Meaning | dictionary.com

Chapter 7

Enchiridion (Epictetus): Book Summary, Key Lessons and Best Quotes (dailystoic.com)

https://dictionary.cambridge.org/us/dictionary/english/peace

Chapter 8

Epictetus quotes · GitHub

Made in the USA
Columbia, SC
16 June 2023

18148776R10074